~A BINGO BOOK~

India
Bingo Book

COMPLETE BINGO GAME IN A BOOK

Written By Rebecca Stark
Educational Books 'n' Bingo

ISBN 978-0-87386-481-7

Educational Books 'n' Bingo

Printed in the U.S.A.

INDIA BINGO DIRECTIONS

INCLUDED:

List of Terms

Templates for Additional Terms and Clues

2 Clues per Term

30 Unique Bingo Cards

Markers

1. **Either cut apart the book or make copies of ALL the sheets. You might want to make an extra copy of the clue sheets to use for introduction and review. Keep the sheets in an envelope for easy reuse.**

2. Cut apart the call cards with terms and clues.

3. Pass out one bingo card per student. There are enough for a class of 30.

4. Pass out markers. You may cut apart the markers included in this book or use any other small items of your choice.

5. Decide whether or not you will require the entire card to be filled. Requiring the entire card to be filled provides a better review. However, if you have a short time to fill, you may prefer to have them do the just the border or some other format. Tell the class before you begin what is required.

6. There are 50 terms. Read the list before you begin. If there are any terms that have not been covered in class, you may want to read to the students the term and clues before you begin.

7. There is a blank space in the middle of each card. You can instruct the students to use it as a free space or you can write in answers to cover terms not included. Of course, in this case you would create your own clues. (Templates provided.)

8. Shuffle the cards and place them in a pile. Two or three clues are provided for each term. If you plan to play the game with the same group more than once, you might want to choose a different clue for each game. If not, you may choose to use more than one clue.

9. Be sure to keep the cards you have used for the present game in a separate pile. When a student calls, "Bingo," he or she will have to verify that the correct answers are on his or her card AND that the markers were placed in response to the proper questions. Pull out the cards that are on the student's card keeping them in the order they were used in the game. Read each clue as it was given and ask the student to identify the correct answer from his or her card.

10. If the student has the correct answers on the card AND has shown that they were marked in response to the *correct questions,* then that student is the winner and the game is over. If the student does not have the correct answers on the card OR he or she marked the answers in response to *the wrong questions,* then the game continues until there is a proper winner.

11. If you want to play again, reshuffle the cards and begin again.

Have fun!

TERMS INCLUDED

Akbar the Great	Hinduism
Aryabhata	independence
Aryans	Indian National Congress
Asia	Indus
aum or om	Jallianwala Bagh
Bangladesh	Muhammad Ali Jinnah
Bollywood	Khyber Pass
Brahmins	Kolkata
Buddha	Kshatriya
Buddhism	Lucknow Pact
caste(s)	mantra
Chandragupta Maurya	monsoon(s)
Deccan Plateau	Mumtaz Mahal
Delhi	Mughal Empire
Dravidians	Mumbai
East India Company	Muslim(s)
The Four Noble Truths	Jawaharlal Nehru
Ganges	nirvana
Indira Nehru Gandhi	Pakistan
Mohandas Gandhi	Sri Ramakrishna
Siddhartha Gautama	Salt March
Great Britain	Sanskrit
Gupta Empire	Sepoy(s)
Hampi	state(s)
Hindi	Veda(s)

Note: Some of the names have alternate spellings not shown here.

Additional Terms

Choose as many other terms as you would like and write them in the squares.
Repeat each as desired. Cut out the squares and randomly distribute them.
Instruct the students to place the square on the center space of their card.

India Bingo

Clues for
Additional
Terms

Write three clues for each of your additional terms.

_____ 1. 2. 3.	_____ 1. 2. 3.
_____ 1. 2. 3.	_____ 1. 2. 3.
_____ 1. 2. 3.	_____ 1. 2. 3.

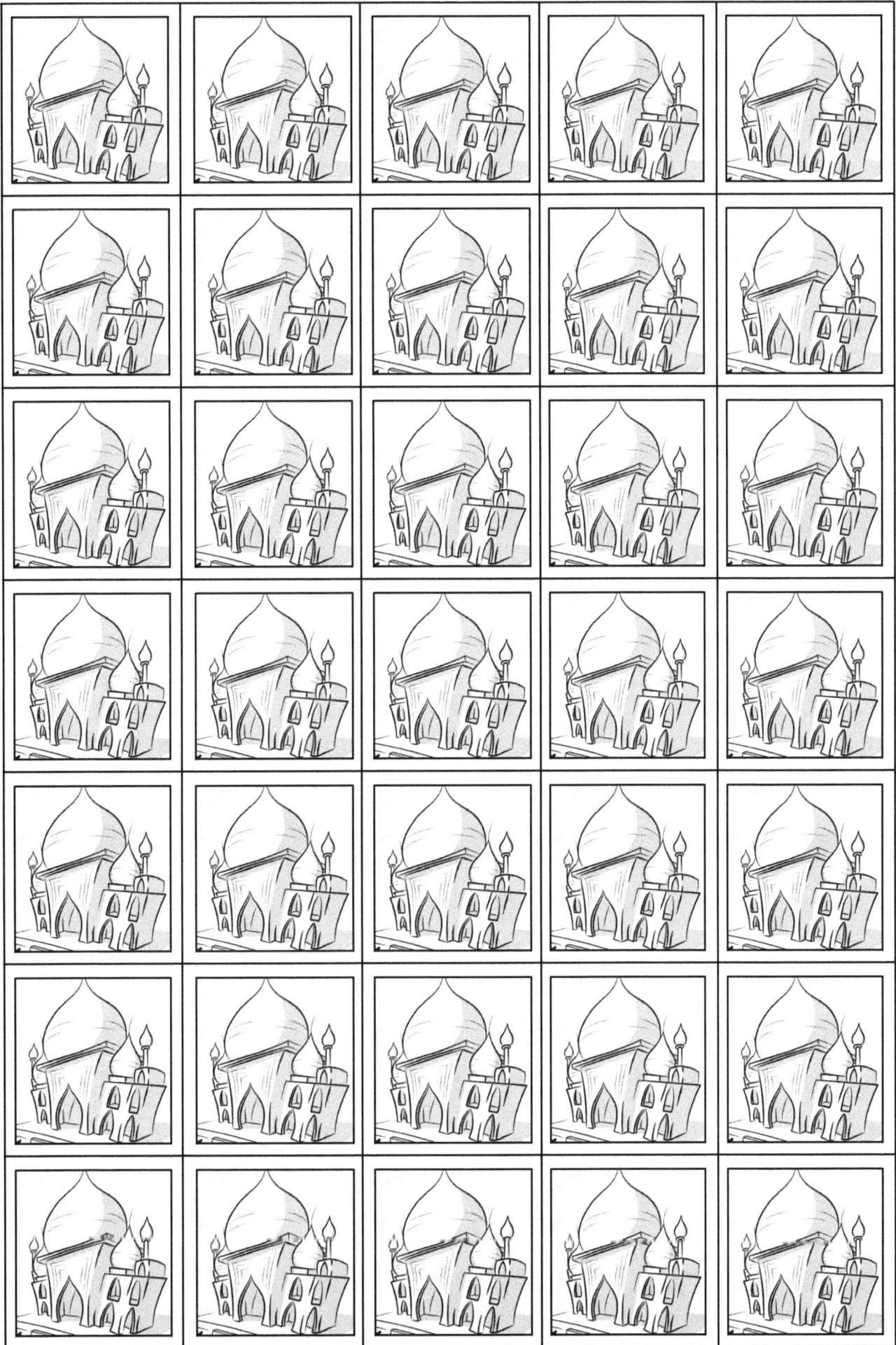

Akbar the Great

1. At fourteen, he led and won the battle to reclaim Delhi from General Hemu.

2. He built the largest army in the history of the Mughal Empire.

3. He lived from 1542–1605 and became ruler of the Mughal Empire at only 13.

Aryabhata

1. This astronomer was born in 476 BCE.

2. His heliocentric theory of gravitation was 1,000 years before that of Copernicus.

3. India's first satellite into orbit was named after him.

Aryans

1. They were a nomadic Indo-European people who entered India by way of the Khyber Pass.

2. They invaded India about 1500 BCE.

3. These nomadic people invented the Sanskrit language.

Asia

1. It is the largest and most populous continent.

2. India is located in this continent.

3. Although India is part of ____, it is often referred to as the subcontinent.

"aum" or "om"

1. It is called the "divine syllable."

2. This divine syllable is the cosmic vibration that is the basis of all existence.

3. This sacred sound is considered the greatest of all mantras.

Bangladesh

1. When East Pakistan seceded, it became ____.

2. ____ is bordered mostly by India.

3. It was once part of British India and then part of Pakistan.

Bollywood

1. It is the nickname for the Hindi-language films industry.

2. It represents only part of the Indian film industry.

3. The name derives from Bombay, the former name for Mumbai, and Hollywood.

Brahmins

1. They are the priests and spiritual class.

2. They are the highest caste in the social hierarchy of the caste system.

3. Members of the Hindu priestly caste are called ____.

Buddha

1. Siddhartha Gautama was known as this.

2. This Sanskrit word means "awakened one."

3. The term sometimes is used to refer someone who embodies divine wisdom and virtue.

India Bingo

Buddhism

1. Siddhartha Gautama was the founder of the religion that became known as ____.

2. The Four Noble Truths and the Eightfold Paths are important parts of this religion.

3. By the 7th century CE, it had the largest following of any religion but later declined.

© Barbara M Peller

caste(s)

1. A ___ is a social status based on class.

2. From highest to lowest the ___ are Brahmins, or priests; Kshatriyas, or kings & warriors; Vaishyas, or merchants & farmers; and Shudras, or laborers.

3. Those outside the ___ system were called Dalits, or untouchables; Gandhi objected to this and called them Harijans, or children of God.

Chandragupta Maurya

1. He was the first Mauryan emperor.

2. ___ unified India.

3. Under Emperor ___ the capital at Patna became a rich and beautiful city.

Deccan Plateau

1. The ___ is a triangular region that makes up most of southern India.

2. The mountains prevent the monsoons from reaching the ___, so it is relatively dry.

3. The name of this region is derived from the Sanskrit word *dakkhin,* meaning "south."

Delhi

1. The Mughal emperor Shah Jahan built Shahjahanabad, now known as Old ___.

2. In 1911 the British shifted their capital from Calcutta to ___.

3. New ___ is the present-day capital of India.

Dravidians

1. These diverse peoples have linguistic similarities.

2. The origin of the name of this linguistic group comes from the Sanskrit term, *darva,* which means "water"or "sea."

3. These indigenous peoples of Southern India and Sri Lanka share any of the 21 variations of the same basic language.

East India Company

1. It was originally formed to pursue trade with the East Indies.

2. It later traded mainly with the Indian subcontinent and China.

3. It was granted a royal charter by Queen Elizabeth I of Great Britain in 1600.

The Four Noble Truths

1. The first, *dukkha,* is sometimes translated as "Life is suffering." It can also refer to anything temporary.

2. The second, *tanha,* teaches that the cause of suffering is craving.

3. The third has to do with the state of *nirvana* and the fourth concerns the Eightfold Path.

Ganges

1. It is officially known by its Hindu name, Ganga Ma.

2. This river is sacred to the Hindus.

3. This river is 1,560 miles (2,510 km) long and flows through China, India, Nepal and Bangladesh.

Indira Nehru Gandhi

1. She was prime minister of India from 1966 to 1977 and from 1980 to 1984.

2. She was prime minister when India sent its first satellite into space.

3. Her father, Jawaharlal Nehru, was the first prime minister of India.

India Bingo

Mohandas Gandhi

1. This non-violent leader of Indian independence became leader of the Indian National Congress in 1921.

2. In 1948 he was assassinated by a fanatic who opposed his program of tolerance.

3. He is known as Mahatma, which means "Great Soul" in Sanskrit.

Siddhartha Gautama

1. Known as Buddha, he is considered the founder of Buddhism.

2. Signs at his birth said that he would be a great king or a great spiritual leader.

3. He became the Enlightened Buddha and wrote the Four Noble Truths.

Great Britain

1. India was ___'s most populous and valuable colony.

2. India gained its independence from ___ in 1947.

3. ___'s Indian Empire was called the British Raj.

Gupta Empire

1. The ___ was founded by Chandra Gupta I, who named himself Maharaja, or King of Kings.

2. It lasted from 320 CE to 550 CE.

3. This time period is often identified as the Golden Age of India.

Hampi

1. Once a remote trading center, ___ became the capital of the Vijayanagar Empire in 1336.

2. ___ was the focus of trade and commerce for southern India during the Sangamas period.

3. Today tourists visit this city for its classical Hindu architecture and art.

Hindi

1. It is the national language of India.

2. This Indo-Aryan language has about 487 million speakers.

3. ___ is called a phonetic language because it is spoken as it is written.

Hindusim

1. ___ includes the belief that there is one absolute God and that other deities are the incarnation of the supreme deity.

2. ___ is one of the oldest of the world's major religions; it began at least as early as 1500 BCE.

3. It teaches that God and nature are one.

independence

1. India gained its ___ from Great Britain in 1947.

2. After World War II, a financially hurting Great Britain agreed to give India its ___.

3. Mahatma Gandhi led a peaceful movement against Great Britain to gain ___.

Indian National Congress

1. It was founded in 1885 to gain economic reforms and a role in decisions made by the Raj.

2. Leaders of the ___ included Mohandas Gandhi and Jawaharlal Nehru.

3. Many Muslims felt they weren't being represented by the Hindu majority and left the ___ to form the Muslim League.

Indus

1. This river begins in the Himalayas in Tibet and empties through its delta into the Arabian Sea.

2. About 1,800 miles (2,896 kilometers) long, it ___ is one of the longest rivers in Asia.

3. This river is now shared by Pakistan and India by treaty agreements.

India Bingo

Jallianwala Bagh

1. A massacre at ___ took place April 13, 1919.

2. The massacre at ___ became a major turning point in India's move toward independence.

3. The Massacre at ___ occurred when Brigadier General Dyer ordered his troops to fire upon crowds of peaceful protesters.

Muhammad Ali Jinnah 1. He is considered the founder and father of the modern nation of Pakistan. 2. In 1947 Pakistan became an independent Muslim nation with ___ as head of state. 3. This leader of Pakistan died in 1948, shortly after the formation of the nation.	**Khyber Pass** 1. Located in the mountains of the Hindu Kush system, the ___ links Pakistan and Afghanistan. 2. This pass has been an important route for traders and invaders. 3. Rudyard Kipling called it "a sword cut through the mountains."
Kolkata 1. Its Anglicized name is Calcutta. 2. It is the largest city in eastern India and is the capital of the state of West Bengal. 3. Located in the Ganges Delta, this city was the seat of the British colonial government in India.	**Kshatriya** 1. This caste comprises kings and warriors. 2. They are second in the social hierarchy of the caste system. 3. Only the Brahmins are a higher social class.
Lucknow Pact 1. This agreement was between the Indian National Congress and the Muslim League. 2. The ___ was a victory for the separatist movement of Muslims in India. 3. The ___ of 1916 granted separate constitutional identity to Muslims.	**mantra** 1. A ___ is a mystical incantation. 2. It is a sacred utterance. 3. The ___ "Aum, Shanti, Shanti, Shanti," meaning "Aum, Peace, Peace, Peace," is found in the *Upanishads.*
monsoon(s) 1. This seasonal wind in southern Asia brings heavy rainfall and causes flooding. 2. The main ___ season in India is from June to September. 3. Mountains protect the Deccan Plateau by preventing the ___ from reaching it.	**Mumtaz Mahal** 1. This was the nickname of Arjumand Banu Begum, Empress of India during the Mughal dynasty. 2. She was the inspiration for the creation of the Taj Mahal. 3. Her husband, Shah Jahan, had the Taj Mahal built as a mausoleum for her.
Mughal Empire 1. Akbar ruled the ___ from 1560 until 1605. 2. Shah Jahan was the ruler of the ___ who built the Taj Mahal 3. Under Akbar the Great, the ___ grew considerably. India Bingo	**Mumbai** 1. This city on the west coast of India used to be called Bombay. 2. It is the most populous city in India. 3. It is the second most populous city in the world. © Barbara M Peller

Muslim(s) 1. The All India ____ League, or AIML, was founded to safeguard the interests of the ____. 2. Tensions between the 2 major religious groups on the Indian sub-continent, the Hindus and the ____, led to Partitioning. 3. Partitioning led two independent states: Hindu India and ____ Pakistan.	**Jawaharlal Nehru** 1. When India was granted independence in 1947, he became the nation's first prime minister. 2. He joined Gandhi in the "salt laws" protests and was arrested several times. 3. His daughter, Indira Ghandi, also became prime minister of India.
nirvana 1. In Buddhism ____ is a state of bliss and selfless enlightenment. 2. The Eightfold Path leads to the attainment of ____. 3. In Buddhism ____ is the state in which one has achieved compassion and release from desire.	**Pakistan** 1. In 1947 ____ became an independent Muslim nation. 2. Muhammad Ali Jinnah was the first head of state of this nation. 3. The partitioning of the Indian subcontinent resulted in the formation of ____.
Sri Ramakrishna 1. This 19-century mystic spent his entire life contemplating the true nature of God. 2. This 19-century mystic believed that one should accept God's will in everything. 3. This mystic taught that God is in everyone and that egoism is the root of all suffering.	**Salt March** 1. The ____ was a reaction to the British Raj's monopoly on salt. 2. Following the ____ Ghandi, and 50,000 others were imprisoned for breaking the salt laws. 3. Despite beatings by police after the ____, no one fought back; it marked the beginning of peaceful resistance.
Sanskrit 1. ____ is the basis of most of India's languages. 2. In ancient India, ____ was taught only to members of the higher castes. 3. The oldest known text in ____, the *Rigveda,* is a collection of over 1,000 Hindu hymns, composed during the 2nd millennium BCE.	**Sepoy(s)** 1. The ____ Rebellion was a mutiny of native Indian troops who had been trained and armed by the British. 2. The ____ Rebellion is also known as India's First War of Independence. 3. The ____ Rebellion is also known as the Indian Rebellion of 1857.
state(s) 1. India comprises 28 ____ and 7 union territories. 2. Mumbai, the most populous city in India, is the capital of the ____ of Maharashtra. 3. Kolkata, the largest city in eastern India, is the capital of the ____ of West Bengal. India Bingo	***Veda(s)*** 1. This collection of religious and philosophical hymns & poems dates from *c.* 3000 BCE. 2. Composed over many generations, the ____ were written in Sanskrit. 3. The oldest and most authoritative Hindu sacred texts, the ____ , were composed in Sanskrit and gathered into 4 collections.

India Bingo

Gupta Empire	Siddhartha Gautama	Hampi	*Veda(s)*	Sanskrit
Brahmins	Akbar the Great	state(s)	Jallianwala Bagh	Great Britain
Jawaharlal Nehru	monsoon(s)		Hindi	Kshatriya
Salt March	Asia	Indira Nehru Gandhi	Pakistan	Hinduism
independence	Buddha	Chandragupta Maurya	Ganges	Mohandas Gandhi

India Bingo

Salt March	nirvana	Indian National Congress	mantra	independence
Hinduism	Jallianwala Bagh	Bangladesh	Asia	Muslim(s)
Mughal Empire	Buddha		Deccan Plateau	Indira Nehru Gandhi
The Four Noble Truths	Mumbai	monsoon(s)	Khyber Pass	Great Britain
Mohandas Gandhi	state(s)	Chandragupta Maurya	Brahmins	Ganges

India Bingo

Salt March	Indira Nehru Gandhi	Jallianwala Bagh	Pakistan	Jawaharlal Nehru
Buddha	Akbar the Great	Aryans	Siddhartha Gautama	Muhammad Ali Jinnah
Asia	state(s)		Muslim(s)	Aryabhata
monsoon(s)	Mughal Empire	independence	The Four Noble Truths	Indian National Congress
Ganges	Brahmins	Chandragupta Maurya	Khyber Pass	Hampi

India Bingo

monsoon(s)	Muslim(s)	independence	Brahmins	Hampi
Indus	Bangladesh	Siddhartha Gautama	mantra	Jawaharlal Nehru
Hindi	The Four Noble Truths		Sanskrit	*Veda(s)*
Indira Nehru Gandhi	East India Company	state(s)	Chandragupta Maurya	Aryans
Dravidians	Mohandas Gandhi	Lucknow Pact	Ganges	Kshatriya

India Bingo: Card No. 4

India Bingo

Mohandas Gandhi	Sanskrit	Asia	Bangladesh	Brahmins
Indus	Indira Nehru Gandhi	Aryans	Deccan Plateau	Akbar the Great
nirvana	Kshatriya		Delhi	caste(s)
Great Britain	Muslim(s)	Gupta Empire	Khyber Pass	Dravidians
Jallianwala Bagh	Chandragupta Maurya	Mumtaz Mahal	monsoon(s)	Hindi

India Bingo: Card No. 5

India Bingo

Aryabhata	Muslim(s)	Indian National Congress	nirvana	Kshatriya
Pakistan	Asia	Dravidians	Siddhartha Gautama	Jawaharlal Nehru
mantra	Aryans		Bangladesh	Deccan Plateau
Chandragupta Maurya	independence	Khyber Pass	Lucknow Pact	Hindi
Hinduism	Indira Nehru Gandhi	Gupta Empire	Mumtaz Mahal	Hampi

India Bingo: Card No. 6

India Bingo

Gupta Empire	Muslim(s)	caste(s)	Delhi	Jallianwala Bagh
Hinduism	Hampi	Buddha	Akbar the Great	Indus
Indian National Congress	*Veda(s)*		Deccan Plateau	Buddhism
monsoon(s)	The Four Noble Truths	Jawaharlal Nehru	Salt March	Mughal Empire
Chandragupta Maurya	Brahmins	Khyber Pass	Lucknow Pact	Aryabhata

India
Bingo

Hindi	Muslim(s)	"aum" or "om"	Pakistan	Buddhism
Indus	nirvana	mantra	Kshatriya	Bangladesh
Jawaharlal Nehru	Kolkata		Hampi	Sanskrit
Ganges	monsoon(s)	Salt March	Dravidians	The Four Noble Truths
state(s)	Chandragupta Maurya	Lucknow Pact	Asia	Hinduism

India Bingo

Deccan Plateau	Jallianwala Bagh	Buddha	Jawaharlal Nehru	Kshatriya
Dravidians	nirvana	Hindi	Asia	Hampi
Muhammad Ali Jinnah	Gupta Empire		Akbar the Great	"aum" or "om"
Buddhism	Mohandas Gandhi	independence	Delhi	caste(s)
The Four Noble Truths	Khyber Pass	Aryans	Salt March	Sanskrit

India Bingo

Salt March	Pakistan	Bangladesh	mantra	Mumtaz Mahal
Kshatriya	Buddhism	Siddhartha Gautama	Akbar the Great	Hampi
Kolkata	Muslim(s)		*Veda(s)*	Mughal Empire
independence	Great Britain	Dravidians	Khyber Pass	Muhammad Ali Jinnah
Bollywood	Hinduism	Indian National Congress	Mohandas Gandhi	Hindi

India Bingo: Card No. 10

India Bingo

Aryabhata	Muslim(s)	Asia	Dravidians	Hinduism
"aum" or "om"	Muhammad Ali Jinnah	Delhi	Deccan Plateau	Siddhartha Gautama
Indus	nirvana		Indian National Congress	Buddha
Bollywood	Jawaharlal Nehru	Khyber Pass	Brahmins	Salt March
Aryans	Chandragupta Maurya	Gupta Empire	Lucknow Pact	Jallianwala Bagh

India Bingo: Card No. 11

India Bingo

Jallianwala Bagh	Sanskrit	Muhammad Ali Jinnah	Pakistan	Deccan Plateau
Buddha	state(s)	nirvana	Lucknow Pact	Akbar the Great
Gupta Empire	caste(s)		Kshatriya	mantra
Chandragupta Maurya	The Four Noble Truths	Hampi	Salt March	Indus
Muslim(s)	"aum" or "om"	Kolkata	Aryans	Buddhism

India Bingo

Bollywood	Sanskrit	Aryabhata	Muhammad Ali Jinnah	Kshatriya
nirvana	"aum" or "om"	Muslim(s)	Deccan Plateau	Mughal Empire
Pakistan	Bangladesh		Buddha	caste(s)
Hindi	Khyber Pass	Buddhism	Kolkata	Salt March
Chandragupta Maurya	Great Britain	Lucknow Pact	Gupta Empire	Delhi

India Bingo

Brahmins	nirvana	Asia	Deccan Plateau	Bollywood
Buddhism	Gupta Empire	Muhammad Ali Jinnah	Akbar the Great	Muslim(s)
Dravidians	*Veda(s)*		Indian National Congress	Aryans
Great Britain	Khyber Pass	Kolkata	Bangladesh	Aryabhata
Chandragupta Maurya	mantra	Mughal Empire	Hinduism	Hindi

India Bingo

Delhi	Deccan Plateau	Asia	Jallianwala Bagh	Pakistan
Aryabhata	Indian National Congress	Siddhartha Gautama	nirvana	Dravidians
Kshatriya	Gupta Empire		Jawaharlal Nehru	Hampi
Chandragupta Maurya	Muhammad Ali Jinnah	"aum" or "om"	Khyber Pass	Bollywood
Hinduism	The Four Noble Truths	Lucknow Pact	Mumtaz Mahal	Buddha

India Bingo

Bangladesh	Muhammad Ali Jinnah	"aum" or "om"	Mumtaz Mahal	Mumbai
mantra	Mughal Empire	caste(s)	Indus	*Veda(s)*
Bollywood	Sanskrit		Kshatriya	Buddha
monsoon(s)	Buddhism	Chandragupta Maurya	Delhi	Salt March
Dravidians	Sepoy(s)	Lucknow Pact	The Four Noble Truths	Muslim(s)

India Bingo

Bollywood	Sri Ramakrishna	East India Company	Muhammad Ali Jinnah	Brahmins
Delhi	Dravidians	Khyber Pass	*Veda(s)*	caste(s)
Deccan Plateau	Salt March		Sepoy(s)	"aum" or "om"
Mohandas Gandhi	Hinduism	Hindi	Asia	Mughal Empire
independence	Aryans	Jallianwala Bagh	Pakistan	Sanskrit

India Bingo: Card No. 17

© Barbara M Peller

India
Bingo

Hampi	Kolkata	Buddhism	Dravidians	mantra
Muslim(s)	Bollywood	independence	Kshatriya	Aryans
Deccan Plateau	Mughal Empire		East India Company	Mumtaz Mahal
Mohandas Gandhi	Siddhartha Gautama	Khyber Pass	Salt March	Indian National Congress
Sepoy(s)	Muhammad Ali Jinnah	Asia	Sri Ramakrishna	Aryabhata

India Bingo: Card No. 18

© Barbara M Peller

India Bingo

Kshatriya	Aryabhata	Muhammad Ali Jinnah	"aum" or "om"	Kolkata
Delhi	Pakistan	Mumtaz Mahal	Jallianwala Bagh	*Veda(s)*
Sri Ramakrishna	Brahmins		Akbar the Great	Hampi
Indian National Congress	Sepoy(s)	independence	The Four Noble Truths	East India Company
Jawaharlal Nehru	Mumbai	Hinduism	Hindi	Lucknow Pact

India Bingo

Kolkata	Sri Ramakrishna	Pakistan	Muhammad Ali Jinnah	Akbar the Great
Bangladesh	Buddha	Indus	independence	mantra
Sanskrit	caste(s)		monsoon(s)	Siddhartha Gautama
Mohandas Gandhi	Hindi	Ganges	The Four Noble Truths	Sepoy(s)
Indira Nehru Gandhi	state(s)	Mumbai	Salt March	East India Company

India Bingo

Delhi	Aryabhata	Indus	Muhammad Ali Jinnah	Great Britain
Sanskrit	East India Company	Buddhism	"aum" or "om"	Gupta Empire
Mughal Empire	Hinduism		Sri Ramakrishna	Asia
independence	Jallianwala Bagh	Sepoy(s)	Mohandas Gandhi	Hindi
monsoon(s)	Mumbai	Lucknow Pact	Bollywood	The Four Noble Truths

India Bingo: Card No. 21

India Bingo

Jawaharlal Nehru	Indian National Congress	East India Company	nirvana	Bollywood
mantra	Pakistan	Hampi	"aum" or "om"	Akbar the Great
Buddhism	*Veda(s)*		Gupta Empire	caste(s)
Sepoy(s)	Mohandas Gandhi	The Four Noble Truths	Siddhartha Gautama	Brahmins
Mumbai	Aryans	Sri Ramakrishna	Mughal Empire	Indus

India Bingo: Card No. 22

India Bingo

Bangladesh	Sri Ramakrishna	Jallianwala Bagh	nirvana	Lucknow Pact
Aryabhata	Kolkata	Hinduism	Delhi	Siddhartha Gautama
Indian National Congress	Bollywood		Ganges	Gupta Empire
Mughal Empire	Mumbai	Sepoy(s)	Aryans	The Four Noble Truths
Great Britain	Hindi	state(s)	independence	East India Company

India Bingo: Card No. 23

India Bingo

Bangladesh	Kolkata	Brahmins	Sri Ramakrishna	"aum" or "om"
Kshatriya	Lucknow Pact	Indus	mantra	Gupta Empire
caste(s)	Mumtaz Mahal		Bollywood	Mughal Empire
Great Britain	Ganges	Sepoy(s)	Aryans	Sanskrit
Indira Nehru Gandhi	monsoon(s)	Mumbai	Pakistan	state(s)

India Bingo: Card No. 24

India Bingo

monsoon(s)	Indus	Sri Ramakrishna	Asia	East India Company
Siddhartha Gautama	Great Britain	Delhi	Bangladesh	Akbar the Great
Sanskrit	"aum" or "om"		Ganges	Sepoy(s)
Mumtaz Mahal	Mohandas Gandhi	state(s)	Mumbai	*Veda(s)*
Lucknow Pact	Brahmins	Buddhism	Dravidians	Indira Nehru Gandhi

India
Bingo

East India Company	Sri Ramakrishna	Ganges	mantra	Mumtaz Mahal
independence	Pakistan	"aum" or "om"	Kolkata	Bangladesh
Great Britain	Indian National Congress		*Veda(s)*	monsoon(s)
Bollywood	nirvana	Mohandas Gandhi	Mumbai	Sepoy(s)
caste(s)	Dravidians	Asia	state(s)	Indira Nehru Gandhi

India Bingo

Ganges	Buddhism	Sri Ramakrishna	Kolkata	Buddha
Great Britain	Indian National Congress	Delhi	Sepoy(s)	Akbar the Great
Khyber Pass	state(s)		Mumbai	monsoon(s)
Mumtaz Mahal	Aryabhata	Indus	Indira Nehru Gandhi	Siddhartha Gautama
Bollywood	*Veda(s)*	East India Company	Jawaharlal Nehru	caste(s)

India Bingo: Card No. 27

India Bingo

Kshatriya	Kolkata	Salt March	Sri Ramakrishna	Buddhism
Buddha	East India Company	Ganges	independence	*Veda(s)*
state(s)	Mughal Empire		Mumtaz Mahal	mantra
caste(s)	Jawaharlal Nehru	Hinduism	Mumbai	Sepoy(s)
nirvana	Deccan Plateau	Bollywood	Indira Nehru Gandhi	Great Britain

India Bingo: Card No. 28

India Bingo

East India Company	Kolkata	Mumtaz Mahal	Delhi	Deccan Plateau
Great Britain	independence	Indus	caste(s)	Jawaharlal Nehru
Sanskrit	Ganges		Akbar the Great	Sri Ramakrishna
Buddha	Mohandas Gandhi	Hampi	Mumbai	Sepoy(s)
Bangladesh	"aum" or "om"	Indira Nehru Gandhi	Aryabhata	state(s)

India Bingo

Brahmins	Sri Ramakrishna	mantra	Deccan Plateau	Sanskrit
Siddhartha Gautama	Mumtaz Mahal	Indian National Congress	*Veda(s)*	Akbar the Great
Indira Nehru Gandhi	Aryans		caste(s)	Indus
Great Britain	Aryabhata	Kolkata	Mumbai	Ganges
Mohandas Gandhi	Jallianwala Bagh	state(s)	East India Company	Hampi

India Bingo: Card No. 30

www.ingramcontent.com/pod-product-compliance
Lightning Source LLC
LaVergne TN
LVHW061337060426
835511LV00014B/1978